AMERICAN COLONIES

Virginia Loh-Hagan

 45TH PARALLEL PRESS

Published in the United States of America by Cherry Lake Publishing Group
Ann Arbor, Michigan
www.cherrylakepublishing.com
Reading Adviser: Marla Conn, MS, Ed., Literacy specialist, Read-Ability, Inc.

Book Designer: Melinda Millward

Photo Credits: © Fotokvadrat/Shutterstock.com, cover, 1; © ESB Essentials/Shutterstock.com, 4; © ZU_09/istockphoto.com, 6; © Morphart Creation/Shutterstock.com, 8; © Joe Sohm/Dreamstime.com, back cover, 10; © Everett Collection/Shutterstock.com, 12; © duncan1890/istockphoto.com, 14; © North Wind Picture Archives / Alamy Stock Photo , 16, 28; © Olivier Le Queinec/Shutterstock.com, 18; © mycteria/Shutterstock.com, 20; © Michael Gordon/Shutterstock.com, 22; © Han_eck/Shutterstock.com, 24; © Historical Images Archive / Alamy Stock Photo , 27

Graphic Element Credits: © Milos Djapovic/Shutterstock.com, back cover, front cover; © cajoer/Shutterstock.com, back cover, front cover, multiple interior pages; © GUSAK OLENA/Shutterstock.com, back cover, multiple interior pages; © Miloje/Shutterstock.com, front cover; © Rtstudio/Shutterstock.com, multiple interior pages; © Konstantin Nikiteev/Dreamstime.com, 29

Library of Congress Cataloging-in-Publication Data

Names: Loh-Hagan, Virginia, author.
Title: American Colonies / by Virginia Loh-Hagan.
Description: Ann Arbor, Michigan : Cherry Lake Publishing, [2021] | Series: Surviving history | Includes index.
Identifiers: LCCN 2020003277 (print) | LCCN 2020003278 (ebook) | ISBN 9781534169128 (hardcover) | ISBN 9781534170803 (paperback) | ISBN 9781534172647 (pdf) | ISBN 9781534174481 (ebook)
Subjects: LCSH: United States—Social life and customs—To 1775—Juvenile literature.
Classification: LCC E162 .L64 2021 (print) | LCC E162 (ebook) | DDC 973.1—dc23
LC record available at https://lccn.loc.gov/2020003277
LC ebook record available at https://lccn.loc.gov/2020003278

Printed in the United States of America
Corporate Graphics

TABLE OF CONTENTS

INTRODUCTION 4

EAT OR STARVE? 8

WAR OR PEACE? 12

FARM OR FAMINE? 16

SICK OR HEALTHY? 20

LIBERTY OR DEATH? 24

SURVIVAL RESULTS 28

DIGGING DEEPER: DID YOU KNOW . . . ? 30

Glossary 32
Learn More! 32
Index 32
About the Author 32

INTRODUCTION

The American colonies were part of the New World.
English language and culture were widely used.

The United States started as 13 British **colonies**. Colonies are areas under the control of another country. The American colonies were established during the 17th and 18th centuries.

American colonists settled along the Atlantic coast. There were 3 groups of colonies. The New England Colonies were the first. They included Connecticut, Massachusetts, New Hampshire, and Rhode Island. The Middle Colonies included Delaware, New Jersey, New York, and Pennsylvania. The Southern Colonies included Maryland, North Carolina, South Carolina, Virginia, and Georgia.

People from Europe **immigrated** to the colonies. Immigrate means to move from another country. These immigrants wanted religious freedom. They wanted land and money. They wanted better lives.

American colonists learned to grow tobacco.
Tobacco was a cash crop.

Not everyone wanted to come. **Slaves** from Africa were sent to the colonies. Slaves are people who are forced to work for free. **Criminals** were also sent to the colonies. Criminals are people who break the law.

American colonists claimed lands. Large families were needed to farm the land. Life was hard. But they learned to live off the land. They started businesses. They became successful.

The colonies made money for Great Britain. They sent goods. They paid taxes. American colonists thought British rule was unfair. They didn't feel like they had a voice. They wanted independence. They fought in a war from 1755 to 1783. It was called the American **Revolution**. Revolution means to overthrow. The colonists won. They formed the United States of America.

EAT OR STARVE?

Captain James Smith traded with local Powhatans for food. Powhatans stopped trading when colonists stole from them.

Jamestown was the first British colony in America. It was in what is now Virginia. About 104 colonists landed in Jamestown. They did this in 1607.

Settling in Jamestown was hard. Summers were hot and humid. Winters were cold. There was a bad winter from 1607 to 1608. This was called the Little Ice Age. There were also **droughts** from 1606 to 1612. Droughts are periods of low rainfall. This meant water was hard to find. Without water, there were no crops. Without crops, there was no food. Without food, people died.

Many colonists **starved** to death during the winter of 1609 to 1610. This was called the starving time. Starve means to die of hunger. Some colonists survived because British ships came with supplies.

QUESTION 1

Would you have starved at Jamestown?

A You didn't want to be the first to go to the New World. You waited. You set sail for the colonies in 1610.

B You were a young and healthy adult. You did what you needed to do to survive. You ate shoe leather. You killed horses. You used wood from your house to make fires.

C You were a child. You got sick. You survived. But your sickness left you weak.

There were only 60 survivors left after the starving time.

SURVIVOR BIOGRAPHY

Phillis Wheatley lived from about 1753 to 1784. She was born in West Africa. She was kidnapped. She was taken on a slave ship. She was sold at age 7 or 8. She was sold to the Wheatley family in Boston. She was smart. She learned to read and write. She learned history and literature. She learned Latin and Greek. She wrote poems. Her first poem was published at age 13. Her poem was about 2 men who almost drowned at sea. Wheatley wrote a book of poems. She became the first African American to publish a book of poetry in the American colonies. She was the third American woman to do so. She was later freed from slavery. She married a freed black man. She had 3 children.

WAR OR PEACE?

There are many different Native American **tribes**.
Tribes are groups of people. These tribes have lived
in the Americas for thousands of years.

American colonists had periods of war and peace with Native Americans. After Jamestown, more colonists came. They spread out. They created new towns. They stole lands away from Native Americans. This led to the American Indian Wars. These wars were fought over many years.

There were many battles. These are 2 examples. From 1636 to 1659, New York colonists fought Native Americans. The battles were violent. Many colonists went back to Europe. From 1756 to 1763, France and Great Britain fought for control of land. Both sides made **alliances** with Native Americans. Alliances are promises to work together. But both countries betrayed Native Americans.

Colonists couldn't be stopped. Native Americans suffered greatly. Their lands and resources were taken. They lost many lives. Their way of life was almost destroyed.

QUESTION 2

How likely was your survival during the American Indian Wars?

A You were a British or American soldier. You had resources. You had training.

B You were a colonist. You were not a fighter. You just wanted to work your land. You depended on Native Americans. Native Americans helped you hunt, fish, and farm.

C You were a Native American. You were left out of peace talks. Your land was taken. You were forced to fight, move, or starve. Colonists brought sicknesses to your people. Some took Native Americans as slaves.

Native Americans had a highly developed system of trade.

SURVIVAL BY THE NUMBERS

- Between 1607 and 1624, about 6,000 to 10,000 colonists came to America. Only 1,275 survived.
- In the early days, about 180 to 200 of every 1,000 children died the first year.
- An average family had about 7 to 8 surviving children.
- By 1750, about 300,000 people lived in New York, New Jersey, and Pennsylvania. Most people lived around the seaports. About 25,000 people lived in Philadelphia. About 15,000 people lived in New York City. About 7,000 people lived in Baltimore.
- In 1775, over 2 million people lived in the 13 colonies. About 500,000 lived in Virginia. Virginia was the largest colony.
- By 1776, about 85 percent of the white settlers came from England, Ireland, Scotland, or Wales. About 9 percent came from Germany. About 4 percent came from Denmark.
- Over 90 percent of colonists were farmers.
- American colonists lived to about 33 to 40 years old.

FARM OR FAMINE?

Farmers' children didn't go to school. They were taught by their parents. Boys got more education than girls.

Famine is an extreme lack of food. Colonists were always at risk for famine. They had to learn to farm. Most colonists were farmers. Farmers worked all year long. Their day started with the sunrise. They needed to use every minute of daylight.

They grew many crops. The types of crops depended on where they lived. Colonial farmers grew wheat. They grew corn. They grew barley. They grew oats. They grew tobacco. They grew rice. Later, colonists grew cotton.

The first colonists didn't own slaves. But by the early 1700s, slaves were forced to work large farms. Only rich people could afford slaves.

QUESTION 3

What type of work would you have done on a colonial farm?

A You were a man. You worked outside. You planted the fields. You gathered the harvest. You took care of farm animals. You chopped wood.

B You were a woman or child. Women made meals. They made clothes. They raised children. Farmers had large families. Children were needed to work farms. Boys helped their fathers. Girls helped their mothers.

C You were a slave. Slaves were kidnapped from their homes in Africa. They had no freedoms. They were treated very badly. They were beaten. They were whipped. They lived in poor conditions.

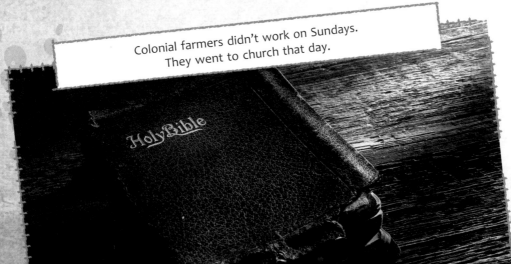

Colonial farmers didn't work on Sundays. They went to church that day.

SURVIVAL TIPS

Follow these tips to survive a famine:

- Be prepared. Learn about weather patterns. Watch for danger signs.
- Check your resources. See what you have.
- Keep a supply of food. Get canned foods.
- Stock up on water. A person needs about a gallon of water a day. Humans can only live 3 days without water.
- Get a first aid kit.
- Grow your own food. Grow foods that don't need a lot of water.
- Stay updated. Listen to the news.
- Don't eat all your food at once. Learn to ration. Ration means to allow yourself to have a fixed amount of food and water.
- Take small bites. Chew slowly.
- Avoid salty foods. Salty foods make people thirsty.
- Save your energy. This reduces your need for food.

SICK OR HEALTHY?

Smallpox was the most feared sickness.
But malaria killed more colonists.

Many poor European immigrants came to the colonies. Slaves from Africa were forced to the colonies. Both groups brought sicknesses with them. For example, they brought **malaria**. Malaria is a deadly fever caused by bug bites. Malaria spread easily in the Southern Colonies. This was due to farming and heavy crowds. Mosquitoes were everywhere. They ate human blood. They laid eggs in water. This spread the sickness.

Colonists faced other sicknesses. **Smallpox** was one of them. It's a sickness that causes fevers and skin rashes. It broke out in Boston. This happened from 1636 to 1698. In 1721, many people left Boston. But they still had the smallpox virus in them. This brought smallpox to the other colonies. Many colonists died from sickness.

QUESTION 4

What would have been your risks of dying from a sickness?

A You were a rich colonist. You could afford to shut yourself away from others. You could afford to leave the city and stay in the country. You could hire doctors. You could buy medicine.

B You were a poor colonist or a slave. You lived in cramped rooms. You were close to other people. You could catch sicknesses. You didn't have money for health care.

C You were a Native American. Your healers knew nothing about foreign sicknesses. You didn't have **immunity**. Immunity is resistance to sickness.

At times, there were many deaths. People had to work day and night to bury the dead.

SURVIVAL TOOLS

American colonists needed candles to see at night. This was a time before electricity. Women made the candles. Candles were made from tallow. Tallow is animal fat. Animals were killed in the fall for meat. That's why women made candles in the fall. They had to make enough candles to last a year. Making candles was hard work. Women dipped cotton wicks over and over again. It took 25 dippings to make 1 candle. Women let the candles cool and harden between dips. They dipped them in big iron pots. The pots had boiling water and melted tallow. The pots were very heavy. Women had to carry them. They had to mix the tallow a lot. They also had to keep the fires going. It took all day to make candles.

LIBERTY OR DEATH?

Colonists called British soldiers Redcoats.

Boston was home to over 2,000 British soldiers. They enforced British rule. They raised taxes. Colonists were angry.

On March 5, 1770, there was a deadly street riot. It started as a small fight. It quickly grew. Colonists threw snowballs, sticks, and stones. They aimed at a group of British soldiers. The soldiers shot at the colonists. They did this without orders. Several colonists were killed.

This event was called the Boston **Massacre**. Massacre means a violent killing. This massacre was used to rally the colonists. It was used to promote the Revolutionary War.

QUESTION 5

Which role would you have played in the Boston Massacre?

A You were a British soldier. You had guns. You were provoked. You defended yourself. Colonists were yelling at you. They threw things at you.

B You were a **loyalist**. Loyalists were colonists. They were loyal to Great Britain. They wouldn't have fought against British soldiers.

C You were a **patriot**. Patriots were colonists. They wanted independence. They fought against British soldiers. When the mob first attacked, church bells rang. This was a signal for patriots to come fight. Patriots joined the mob.

Crispus Attucks was half-black and half-Native American.
He was the first to die in the Boston Massacre.

SURVIVAL RESULTS

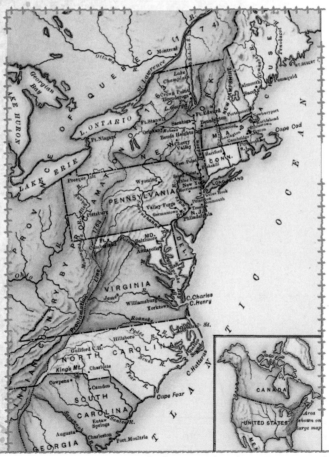

Many colonies were named after British rulers. For example,
New York was named after the Duke of York.

Would you have survived?

Find out! Add up your answers to the chapter questions. Did you have more **A**s, **B**s, or **C**s?

- If you had more **A**s, then you're a survivor! Congrats!

- If you had more **B**s, then you're on the edge. With some luck, you might have just made it.

- If you had more **C**s, then you wouldn't have survived.

Are you happy with your results? Did you have a tie? Sometimes fate is already decided for us. Follow the link below to our webpage. Scroll until you find the series name *Surviving History*. Click download. Print out the template. Follow the directions to create your own paper die. Read the book again. Roll the die to find your new answers. Did your fate change?

https://cherrylakepublishing.com/teaching_guides

DIGGING DEEPER: DID YOU KNOW...?

Living in the American colonies was exciting. American colonists achieved great things. But many lives were lost as well. Surviving history involves many different factors. Dig deeper. Consider some of the facts below.

QUESTION 1:

Would you have starved at Jamestown?

- Colonists relied on trading with Native Americans.
- Colonists relied on supplies from England.
- Several English ships sank before getting to Jamestown.

QUESTION 2:

How likely was your survival during the American Indian Wars?

- Some colonists paid Native Americans to work for them.
- Some Native Americans fought in the American Revolution. They took sides.
- Native Americans thought no one could own land. They lived with nature.

QUESTION 3:

What type of work would you have done on a colonial farm?

- Farmers with money could buy an ox or horse. Poorer farmers had to do everything themselves.
- Some farmers bought women to be their wives.
- Two main classes seemed to develop: rich landowners and poor farmers.

QUESTION 4:

What would have been your risks of dying from a sickness?

- The first medical school was founded in Philadelphia in 1765.
- Lack of proper food made people weak. It made people get sick more easily.
- Native Americans had no experience with outside sicknesses. They couldn't protect themselves.

QUESTION 5:

Which role would you have played in the Boston Massacre?

- British soldiers were given a fair trial.
- British soldiers left Boston. They went to Fort William.
- Leading patriots included Paul Revere and Samuel Adams.

GLOSSARY

alliances (uh-LYE-uhns-iz) partnerships formed for a specific purpose

colonies (KAH-luh-neez) areas under the control of another country

criminals (KRIM-uh-nuhlz) people who break laws

droughts (DROUTS) periods of low rainfall

famine (FAM-in) extreme lack of food

immigrated (IM-uh-gray-tid) moved from a country to settle in another country

immunity (ih-MYOON-ih-tee) resistance to diseases

loyalist (LOI-uhl-ist) colonist who was loyal to Great Britain

malaria (muh-LAIR-ee-uh) a deadly disease with fevers caused by mosquito bites

massacre (MAS-uh-kur) a violent killing

patriot (PAY-tree-uht) colonist who wanted independence from Great Britain

revolution (rev-uh-LOO-shun) a forcible overthrow of a government

slaves (SLAYVZ) people who are forced to work for free

smallpox (SMAWL-pahks) a deadly disease that causes fevers and skin rashes

starved (STAHRVD) died of hunger

tribes (TRYBZ) groups of people

LEARN MORE!

- Morley, Jacqueline, and David Antram (illust.). *You Wouldn't Want to Be an American Colonist!* New York, NY: Franklin Watts, 2013.
- Raum, Elizabeth. *The Scoop on Clothes, Homes, and Daily Life in Colonial America*. North Mankato, MN: Capstone Press, 2017.
- Vonne, Mira. *Gross Facts About the American Colonies*. North Mankato, MN: Capstone Press, 2017.

INDEX

Adams, Samuel, 31
African Americans, 11, 18
alliances, 13
American colonies
    overview, 5, 7
    statistics, 15
American Indian Wars, 13, 14, 30
American Revolution, 7, 25, 30
Attucks, Crispus, 27

Boston Massacre, 25, 26, 27, 31
British soldiers, 24, 25, 26, 31

candles, 23
children, 10, 15, 16, 18
colonies, 5

colonists, 13, 14, 15, 25, 26, 30
criminals, 7

deaths, 9, 21, 22, 27, droughts, 9

famine, 17, 19
farmers/farming, 15, 16–18, 31

Great Britain, 7

immigrants, 5, 21

Jamestown, 9, 10, 13, 30

landowners, 31
loyalists, 26

malaria, 20, 21
Middle Colonies, 5
mosquitoes, 21

Native Americans, 12–14, 22, 30, 31
New England Colonies, 5
New World, 4, 10

patriots, 26, 31
Powhatans, 8

Redcoats, 24
Revere, Paul, 31
Revolution, American, 7, 25, 30
riots, 25

sickness, 14, 20–22, 31
slaves, 7, 17, 18, 21, 22

smallpox, 20, 21
Smith, James, 8
soldiers, 14, 25, 31
soldiers, British, 24, 25, 26, 31
Southern Colonies, 5
starvation, 9, 10, 30
survival tips, 19
survivors, 10, 15

taxes, 25
tobacco, 6
tools, survival, 23

United States of America, 7

wars, 13, 14, 30
Wheatley, Phyllis, 11
women, 18, 23, 31

ABOUT THE AUTHOR

Dr. Virginia Loh-Hagan is an author, university professor, and former classroom teacher. She was born and raised in Virginia, the first American colony. She lives in San Diego with her very tall husband and very naughty dogs. To learn more about her, visit www.virginialoh.com.